The Butterfly Transformation

By Kendra Cordova

Copyright © 2020 Kendra Cordova

All rights reserved. This book or any portion thereof may not be reproduced or used in any manner without the express written permission of the author except for the use of brief quotations in a book review.

Paperback ISBN 978-1-7322121-6-9

Cover Art: Kendra Cordova

This book is dedicated to the challenges that I've overcome. You showed me how to be strong.

Table of Contents

My Story	1
<u>The Caterpillar Stage</u>	3
Change and Transformation	4
Loss and Forgiveness	9
*Caterpillar Exercises	14
<u>The Chrysalis Stage</u>	16
Fear and Courage	17
Pain and Healing	21
*Chrysalis Exercises	23
<u>The Butterfly Stage</u>	25
Control and Freedom	26
*Butterfly Exercises	29
A Butterfly's 10 Tips for Healing	33
About the Author	44

My Story

I wrote this book for people like me. The people who have had their world turned upside down by disease, loss, or other painful life events. I wrote this book because I want you to know that you are not alone. And, even if everything seems dark right now, there is hope.

I'm in my 20s, and up until the beginning of 2019, my life was pretty normal. I was just another military spouse with a young child and another one on the way. I had been a dance teacher, I was physically active, and my health was pretty good...or so I had thought.

A few months into my pregnancy with my daughter, my joints started to hurt and swell. Over the course of a few weeks, I developed rashes, my muscles became weak and sore, I was fatigued all the time, and I started losing my hair.

It was determined that, although my bloodwork came back as normal, my physical symptoms were those of a lupus-like autoimmune disease. But the doctors were hopeful that because it had started during my pregnancy, once I gave birth to my daughter, my symptoms could just go away.

They didn't. I still have days when I can barely walk, and I need to use a cane. I am still losing my hair. I am still in pain a lot of the time, and I am on a handful of medications, plus weekly injections. I will have this for the rest of my life.

And yet…

I'm happier now than I've ever been. I smile more. Colors seem brighter, and I really enjoy my life and my time again.

This is all because of my own personal butterfly transformation. It's a healing process, and I will go through it step-by-step in this book.

I found real happiness, but it took a tremendous transformation within myself. I had to adapt to the painful change that I was given.

And you can, too.

The Caterpillar Stage

We all start off as a caterpillar. We are simply going about our day-to-day life, with no idea of what is to come. We might not be happy, but we are comfortable. However, we can't stay there forever. Not after things start to fall apart. When our lives change, we must change, too.

But while the event that changed us might be painful, the change within ourselves doesn't have to be a bad one. It can make us stronger and more beautiful. Personal transformation can turn us into the best version of ourselves. The caterpillar doesn't practice flying, and yet, that is its destiny.

We will go through the butterfly transformation many times in our lives because our lives are constantly changing. Each time it will feel a little different, and it won't necessarily get any easier; however, when you break it down into steps, it can become clearer that these changes are nothing more than a personal life transformation.

Change and Transformation

The word "change" can make us anxious. This is because it comes with an uncertainty, and a reminder that things are no longer the same as they used to be. Often, change comes without our choice. When things change, it reminds us that our lives are not as stable as we thought, and that we are not really in control of anything outside of ourselves.

Just like when you drive to the store, you are only in control of your own car. Not the weather, not the driving conditions, not the traffic, and not the other drivers. Only yourself. This, too, is how our lives work in every aspect, from work to our love life to our health. There are things within us that we can control, but we can't control others. This is important to remember as we move forward into our butterfly life.

But what if, instead of the word "change," we used the word "transformation"? Transformation signifies a change for the better. Transformation gives the power back to us, like when we post photos on social media of our body transformations or side-by-side photos of how we have changed over a decade of time. When we share these images, we are showing others how we have reached our goals and how we have grown over time.

Transformation is a change. It is a change that we consciously worked on and made happen for ourselves. And this is where our power lies. Things outside of us will continue to change, just like the seasons do. We can't control that. But we can control ourselves and our own changes: we can create our own transformations.

I had dealt with change in some form or another my entire childhood. I had grown up in a military family, which meant moving around from place to place every few years. But when I was 14, I had my first real taste of a big life change. And for me, at the time, it was devastating.

I had started ballet when I was only 2 years old. And while I had continued to try different kinds of dance as I grew up, ballet was my passion. I started in my pointe shoes when I was only 9, and when I turned 14, I decided that I wanted to be a professional ballerina. This meant that at the end of high school, I would have to audition for a company.

I had a little less than four years to become the best I could be. However, in the spring, everything changed for me. During one of my advanced dance classes, we were doing barrel turns at the end of class. They were a challenge for everyone, but I was one of the few students who could execute them almost perfectly. When it was my turn, I took my place and started to leap.

1…I counted in my head as I spun in the air…2…my bare feet pushed me off the cement floor into the next trick…3…I landed on the side of my left foot, and my ankle snapped down. I hit the ground and looked up at the lights on the ceiling. For a moment, everything stood still. And then, as I sat up, the pain hit me.

I had torn three ligaments in my ankle. Because of the injury, I was on crutches for three months and had six months of physical therapy. The physical therapists did everything they could to try and get me back up on my pointe shoes, but it was no use. Even though my ligaments had healed, and my ankle was strong again, the injury had given me nerve damage. It was irreversible, and I could no longer point my toes or go up on my pointe shoes.

However, for a long time, I fought this fact. I tried desperately to hang onto my caterpillar life. But no matter how many hours I put into rehearsal, no matter how much I tried to push up onto my shoes, I just couldn't anymore. I danced one more solo, "The Dying Swan Variation," and was lucky enough to place in the top ten at a competition that year. But that dance was my farewell to ballet. That was the last time I put on a tutu.

Once I let go of my identity as a ballerina, I was able to find joy and passion in different arts, which I hadn't previously had much time for. I didn't have my ankle, but I could still walk. And I still had the rest of my body. So, I put focus into drawing and painting, I fell in love with the theater, and I learned how to do two new kinds of dance that didn't require my ankle: ballroom and belly dancing.

These were skills that I was able to enjoy for years afterward and that I carried into my adulthood. I spent some time as an art instructor, I performed in both college and community theaters, and I danced in a professional ballroom competition with a good friend of mine. I had even healed enough of my heart to spend some time as a dance teacher, and two of the classes that I taught were ballet.

I used to think that I would hate dance forever after my accident, and that ballet had somehow betrayed me. But that was not the case. Things change, and we must change along with them if we want to find happiness. Joy can be found all around us. But we can't keep looking for it in the same places that we did as a caterpillar. Instead, we must look for it where the butterflies are.

We must take the change we are given and turn it into a transformation.

Loss and Forgiveness

Sometimes the change that we experience is in the form of the death of someone we love. This, while a natural part of life, can be the most painful of all the life changes that we go through. The people close to us help us find the joy in life, and they create lasting memories with us. They are there to support us and remind us of our beauty and strength. But when they are gone, it can feel like there is a hole in our lives, and it can make it difficult to enjoy the same things that we used to.

The loss we experience can also be in the form of the loss of a job, our house, or a breakup. Whatever the reason for the loss, all are life-changing. Loss leaves an empty space in our lives, and often has us asking ourselves: What will I do now?

Pain and despair are both expected feelings when we experience loss. However, there is one feeling associated with loss that many people don't warn us about: anger. It can come as anger with yourself, anger with the person who died, or even anger with God or the universe.

An example of a time I experienced this was when I had my first symptom of my autoimmune disease. I went to bed on the night of February 12, 2018, like any other night. At the time, I was 12 weeks pregnant. A month prior, I had seen my baby's heartbeat on an ultrasound. But when I woke up in the early morning of the 13th with pain in my stomach...I was bleeding, and I was no longer pregnant. My baby was gone. I had miscarried.

At the time, when this happened, I had no idea that it was connected to my disease, because it wasn't until a year later that I found out that I had an autoimmune disease. For weeks after my miscarriage, I cried and blamed myself, thinking that I must have done something wrong to cause it.

But the truth is that I had done everything right. I ate healthy, stayed active, and took my vitamins. What happened was out of my control. When they ran tests in the hospital, they couldn't find a reason for the miscarriage. The doctor in the ER had simply said, "These things just happen sometimes."

And that is the truth.

Death happens. Loss happens. It is out of our control. So, how do we turn this into a transformation? How can something so painful bring more joy into our lives?

Two things can transform loss: forgiveness and gratitude.

First, we must forgive ourselves. We need to be kind and understanding with ourselves for the way that we feel and allow our feelings to flow through us as they come. Even those of us who are often sympathetic towards others can be very harsh on ourselves. But this is the time to heal. You must extend the same kindness to yourself that you would give a friend of yours who was grieving.

Second, we must forgive others. Especially the person whom we lost. Sometimes, if they died from something like smoking or drinking, we can hold that against them, and we will feel angry that they are gone. We will feel abandoned, like they left us on purpose, or like they meant to hurt us.

We will never be able to heal if we continue to hold onto our anger with them, because those actions of theirs that led to their cause of death are in the past. That time is part of your caterpillar life, and it will not have a place in your butterfly life. It is over now.

Lastly, we must make peace with the universe. Loss by accident or disease can make us feel like we are somehow cursed or that we have somehow upset the divine energies, and now they are out to get us. But the truth is that death and loss are just as natural as breathing or the phases of the moon. Death is not a punishment. It is simply a part of our own seasons and cycles.

Once we have finally allowed ourselves to express forgiveness, there is another step that we must take. It is essential to move into our new life and transform ourselves so that we learn to focus on gratitude. As a caterpillar, you saw only certain areas of life. But now, with this new life experience, you can see things in a new way. And this new sight, this butterfly view, is the beautiful gift that we are given, even from the most painful situations.

The healing power of gratitude was something I discovered once I forgave myself for my miscarriage. Time with my son became even more precious than before, because having him in my life felt like an even greater gift now. And at the time of the miscarriage, I was a dance teacher. My students were like my kids. Teaching them and having fun at the dance studio made my day even brighter when I returned to work, and I was so thankful for my job and for my students.

So many of us take the people in our lives for granted. We forget what a blessing it is to have the things that we have in life...until they are taken away. This is the lesson of loss. People who have experienced loss have a deeper understanding of the subtle miracles around us and how special our time together really is.

And here is the other important lesson to transform our loss into joy: We had those special people in our lives. We had that place or that job that we lost. Even if they don't have a place in our new life...we had it. And that was a blessing.

This feeling of gratitude for what we have had in our lives, even if it is no longer with us, is where our first seeds of transformation can take root. This joy we feel from our memories, and the thankful feelings they create, can serve as the sunlight starting to peek through the rainclouds that have fogged up our eyes.

Now, with the bright sun coming out, we will be able to see all the beautiful things in our lives again.

Caterpillar Exercises

*Note: You might want to dedicate a special journal or notebook to the exercises you will find throughout this book. Also, you can do all the exercises if you would like, but you can also just pick one or two from each stage of transformation.

Thank You Letter

This new life change might have shaken everything up and caused you some pain. But it has taught you valuable new lessons. Write a thank you letter to the life change and tell it all the good that has come because of it. (Even if there is only one small thing.)

Example: Thank you, miscarriage, for reminding me how precious my children are, and for letting me know that even if it is difficult, I can get pregnant. This gives me hope for the future.

This might be a difficult exercise, and it might feel a bit strange to say thank you for something awful. However, it will help you to get into a thankful mindset.

Post Card to the Past

This is a 'wish you were here' card to your old caterpillar self. Tell your old self all the wonderful things you still have, and what you are looking forward to right now. Even if it is something as simple as the weather outside or a new sweater. Just talk about the future like it is a vacation and tell your old self what they have to look forward to.

Butterfly Perspective

Now that your life has changed in some way, you have a new perspective you can see from. Make a list of five things that you can see differently now, and how this new view on things can help you from now on.

The Chrysalis Stage

Now we are officially letting go of our caterpillar life. The chrysalis stage is the stage of active transformation. Here, we might not be used to our butterfly life yet, but we are moving towards it. We are allowing ourselves to change.

In this stage, we feel different. And, although we aren't sure who we will be at the end of it all, we are embracing our new life, and the new us.

We are finally beginning to heal.

Fear and Courage

The first time that I was truly afraid of what might happen to me because of my disease was in April of 2019. I'd already been dealing with two months of joint and muscle pain with some rashes. But I could cover the rashes with makeup. And while my joints were a bit red and swollen, overall, I looked pretty normal.

But one morning, while I was getting ready, I thought my hair had dried weird because it wouldn't clip back the way it usually would. I reached my hand up to smooth back a frizzy bit in the front of my hairline...but my fingers barely touched any hair. I rubbed my fingers along the spot, and it was mostly skin because the hair was so thin.

Tears welled up in my eyes as I looked back at my reflection in the mirror. My hairline was receding on one side of my head. And within a few weeks, I had multiple thinning sections all over my head. I no longer only felt sick...now I even looked sick. Every time I washed my hair in the shower, I had to spend extra time rinsing loose pieces of hair from my hands and shoulders.

I could no longer deny what was happening. And this is a major step in the chrysalis stage. In this stage, we must face our life change head on. As a caterpillar, this thing happened to us, and it changed everything. But here, in the chrysalis stage, we have an active role in what happens now.

I could feel my active role when I was in the waiting room for yet another doctor's appointment. I was going to see rheumatology, but this time it felt strange because it was my birthday. I had never spent my birthday at the doctor's office, and part of me wondered if this was going to become my new normal.

Suddenly, a wave of fear washed over me, and I wanted to run. I wanted to stand up, walk out of the waiting room, and never come back. I didn't want to be sick, and part of me felt that if I told myself I wasn't sick, everything would just go back to normal.

This moment is when I had to find the courage to take an active role in my future. I couldn't control whether I was sick or not, but I could make choices to take care of myself and get the medical care I needed. I could agree to take care of myself so that

I could have more time to play with my kids and enjoy the good days when I wasn't in as much pain.

Even now, I know that I can't control if I will be able to walk without a cane tomorrow. I can't control how much hair I lose. And I can't control how long this flare will last. But every day that I wake up, I am given the opportunity to enjoy another day, even if that means nothing more than cuddling with my kids on the couch and watching movies all day together or reading books with them in bed.

I am in control of my personal choices and how I choose to spend the time I am given. Yes, there are some limitations, but I still have a lot to be thankful for...and I am very grateful for every little bit of it.

Transforming fear into courage is about facing the truth about what we can't control, while also having the courage to take action on the things we can control.

We can make a difference in our lives, and we can reclaim our power if we just have the courage to take that first step.

Pain and Healing

There is a second wave of pain that we must face when we come to the chrysalis stage. Now that we have the courage to face our fears, we are going to have a deeper understanding of how permanent this new life is. There will be days when you will feel happy again during this stage, but there are also going to be days when you encounter a new obstacle that will remind you of how different your life is now, and your pain will come back.

This part of the chrysalis stage hit me right after I gave birth to my daughter. I was given a stress dose of steroids during the delivery. It completely erased my joint swelling, and my muscles didn't hurt anymore. It was the most normal I had felt in months. I held my daughter in my arms...and I was so happy.

The doctors had told me that there was a chance that my sickness would go away after I had my baby. Perhaps my illness was a strange reaction to my pregnancy. But there was a part of me that wasn't so sure. Something about my body felt different still.

I can remember sitting in the hospital room late one night, looking down at my hands, which were no longer swollen. My daughter was sleeping next to me, and I remember wondering if I would always be able to hold her without pain. I wanted the last few months to be nothing more than a bad dream, and to take my baby home, and go on playing and cuddling with her like I had after my son was born.

And for a little while, I did. But it didn't last long. Within about a week, my rashes, joint swelling, muscle weakness, and other symptoms started to come back. This caused the pain and tears from earlier to hit me again.

The key to healing in the chrysalis stage is by taking active steps to change your focus from what you CAN'T do anymore, and instead, turn your gaze towards all the things you CAN do.

Your life might be changing...
BUT SO ARE YOU.

Chrysalis Exercises

I Can't...But I Can...

To help you transition into your new butterfly life, you must start looking at the things you can do, even if all hope seems lost. For this activity, divide your paper into two lists. On one side, list the things that have been giving you pain, the things you miss, or the things you can no longer do. Then, on the other side, for every item on the list that you can't do, write an alternative or something that you can do.

*Can't Do: *Can Do:

Every time one of the things under "Can't Do" comes to mind in the next few weeks, look at your list for the positive thing you "Can Do".

A Charming Reminder

Sometimes we need a reminder of the wonderful things we have. Out of sight out of mind even applies to our blessings. During life transitions, it is even more important to keep the things we love close to us. And this is how this exercise will help you during this transition period.

As a reminder to yourself of the things that make you happy, you can start a charm bracelet. There are three types of charms to put on your bracelet: people/places you love, things that make you smile, and motivational words.

Examples of charm ideas: a pawprint for a pet, or baby feet for your kids...a cactus from out west or dolphins from the beach...musical notes, teacups...or charms that say things like "be strong". And don't forget a butterfly charm to represent your transformation!

Wear this every day, and it will help remind you of your blessings when you feel down or alone.

The Butterfly Stage

Now is the time to spread your wings, butterfly! Your life has changed, and you have started to take action to grow into your new life. But now comes the big question: Who do you want to transform into? What is your butterfly self like?

While the changes you've gone through might not have been your choice, you DO have power over your personal transformation.

You are in control of the new you. You have a different view of your life now as a butterfly. You can see things differently as you flap above the ground with your new wings. But now that you have been gifted with this new sight, you have new opportunities and new places you can go.

So, where do you want to go?

Control and Freedom

You can't fly until you let go of your need for control. And the truth is, you were never really in control. As I said earlier in the book, the only thing you can control is yourself. You can't go back to your caterpillar life, but you can choose to fly now as a butterfly. Now that things are different, you can do things differently.

Freedom is power, and this includes freedom from our own binds that we put on ourselves. To truly be free to fly into our new butterfly lives, we have to change our mentality about who we are and what we can do.

So, who do you want to be? If there were no expectations or rules put on you, what would your life look like? What would you wear? Where would you go? What makes you happy?

At first, the things that come to mind might feel like they are silly, or you might be afraid to fully embrace these ideas or lifestyle changes. You might think that they are impossible...but who says they are? You just recently had a life-changing event (as bad as it may have been), and you might not have thought something like that would ever happen...but it did. And who is to say that good and wonderful life-changing events can't also happen to you?

This is where you CAN take control of things. You have control over your actions, how you spend your time, and how you express yourself. If there is something you want to add to your new life or something that you want to try, all you have to do is start taking steps towards it. Even if it is only one little step at a time, you have the power to move yourself towards your goals.

And you are free to do so. Yes, other people might think it's crazy, or get angry, or not understand you...but their reaction is not something you have control over. And they don't have control over you. This is just another imaginary bind that we put on ourselves. The only person who has to live with your choices is YOU!

The shocking pain of learning that I might have a shorter lifespan because of my disease was what taught me these lessons. Now, not only will I have days where I am in pain and sick, but I am at a higher risk for things like cancer, kidney failure, and other diseases.

So, I thought to myself: I might as well do what I want to do right now while I can, right? I don't know how many years I'll be able to do as much as I can now. I changed my style a bit to help me feel pretty on my sick days. I started planning those road trips that I had been putting off. And, I started writing this book because I had been wanting to share my voice and my story...and so I did.

But not everybody will understand why you are doing things a little differently...and that's okay! They don't have to. Now, I don't mean to simply ignore people's feelings or shrug off other people all the time. What I AM saying is that not every choice you make has to be about other people. Your hair is your hair, your clothes are your clothes, and how you spend your time is YOUR CHOICE.

Let go of controlling other people, and instead, control your own actions.

Set yourself free from the binds you have put on yourself and fly away into the freedom of your butterfly life!

Butterfly Exercises

I AM

For this exercise, make a list of 10 "I am" statements to say every morning. Pick things you want to be (even if you don't feel that way, yet). Good examples are things like: I am happy, I am confident, I am beautiful…etc.

The more you say it, the more it will feel true…*and the more it will become true!*

Your Butterfly List

As I explained in the butterfly chapters, this part of the healing process allows you to step into your power and shape your new life. This list will help you get started. There are two steps:

-First, make a list of 5 things you envision in your life. You can say things like: a new job, smiling more often, eating healthier, etc.

-Then, for every item, list at least one small step you can take to work towards incorporating that new vision in your life.

Keep this list by your bed, taped to your mirror, in your wallet, or somewhere you will look at it often. When you feel like things aren't going the way you would like, instead of wondering why...look at your list and see what you can do to change it.

A Physical Transformation

Things are different now. And because of this, sometimes looking at the old rooms, your old clothes, or other things that remind you of the past can become very painful. It can pull us back to the feelings from our caterpillar stage.

However, a physical change of some sort can put you into this 'new life' mentality. It can boost your confidence, give you a sense of comfort, or remind you that you can have a fresh start.

An obvious example is something like moving to a new town or getting a haircut, but for some people this might feel a bit drastic. You can also make this physical change by trying some of these more simplistic options:

-Redecorate a room in your house.

-Try a new restaurant.

-Donate old clothes and update your wardrobe.

-Try a new soap or perfume.

-Pick up a new hobby like painting or yoga.

-Start volunteering your time once a week.

-Start reading a new book series.

There are many other ideas that I'm sure you can think of. It's important to pick one that feels therapeutic, brings you joy, and reminds you that change can be a good thing. Life is still beautiful.

Welcome to your butterfly life.

A Butterfly's 10 Tips for Healing

1. Choose Happy

Have you seen those statues of the fat Buddha figure? The story behind him is beautiful, and I added him to my charm bracelet to remind me how easy it is to spread joy. He is based on a monk who traveled from town to town, and instead of preaching or talking with people, he simply smiled and laughed everywhere he went.

And it worked! He spread happiness and laughter, and all he had to do was share a smile and laugh along with others. Smiling has a healing effect on us, and it is contagious. When we smile, it brightens our own energy, as well as lifting up those around us. And when they smile back at us, it aids in our healing…and the cycle goes on.

2. <u>Heal Yourself First</u>

We often try to run around and fix everything in our lives. We want to help our significant other, our family, our friends, clean our house, do a good job at work, etc…and yet, as hard as we try, we can't ever seem to catch up on everything. Something always seems to be falling apart.

This is because WE are still unbalanced. We are in pain, exhausted, and stressed. The people in your life need you to be at your best, and you can't help them if you're broken, too. Re-energize yourself! Take care of yourself. And give yourself the same love and care you would want for those around you.

You can take a break from a busy schedule, get some extra sleep, or find some time this week to do something that YOU like to do. Once you are feeling more energized, it will show. Those around you will be able to tell, and you will not only be able to help them more now, but they will also be happy to see you doing so well.

3. Shine Your Unique Light

Your story is unique. And while you are not alone in your struggles, your exact experiences and the way you are living through them is what makes them YOUR experiences. You are the best and only version of YOU out there…and the world needs you to be you!

Sometimes we find ourselves keeping our opinions to ourselves or acting/dressing/speaking in a certain way in order to avoid confrontation from the people around us, especially our families. But this deprives the world of our talents and gifts. It blocks opportunities for our own personal growth, as well as the opportunities we are given to be a light of inspiration for others.

An important part of life is to allow yourself more personal expression. Things sometimes happen that bring us pain. However, one of the best ways to bring joy to our lives (and the lives of those we love) is to be our *genuine selves*.

4. Life is Cyclical

You will go through the butterfly transformation many times in your life. We are a part of nature, and nature has cycles. The seasons, the moon, the weather, life and death…everything is a cycle. We will go through healing cycles, as well.

It's okay to transform as we heal. If something isn't working for you anymore, it's okay to let it go. Try new things and grow into new ideas. The version of you that you are today is different than you used to be, and the version of you tomorrow, or even years from now, is going to be different, too. We will transform as we have new experiences and learn new information about ourselves and the world around us.

What might feel like the end of something might be the beginning of something new. But we can't really see where this change stands in our life cycle until we enter another part of the cycle and can look back on it. Because of this, we must trust the ups and downs we go through and live in the moment instead of trying to fix everything. *The bad times will come and go, but we must live now.*

Take a sip of some hot cocoa in the winter and watch the quiet snowfall outside. The trees are not dead forever, so take comfort in the coming springtime when it seems cold and dark. So, too, will your sadness turn into joy. When you are down, take care of yourself, and gaze out over your situation with the knowledge that the happiness and the light will return again. As it always does.

Everything is a cycle.

Nothing lasts forever.

But that is the magic of life…

It's this constant transformation that allows us to become a butterfly.

5. Nature Heals Us

We are a part of nature. In our modern world where we are constantly surrounded by smart phones, buzzing computers, florescent lights, and concrete…it can be easy to forget that our bodies and souls are part of the natural world.

When we go through major life changes and we need a place of refuge and healing, there is no better place than nature. Even meditating on something as simple as a potted plant in our kitchen can boost our spirits. So, take a walk in the park or sit outside on your porch and let the wind blow away your stress. Stand barefoot on the earth or listen to the rain on your windowpane.

These sounds, sights, scents, and feelings will awaken your DNA. They will uplift your soul and remind you of the cyclical nature of all things. *Our lives have seasons just like the Earth, and when we reconnect with that part of us, we are healed.*

6. Admire Each Unique Flower

Our world is full of beautiful diversity, and diversity is the spice of life. In your new butterfly life, you will come into contact with many different types of people and situations. Because your life has changed so drastically, it will be much easier to see the diversity of life around you.

There is no need to be afraid of change anymore, now that you have learned how to grow through it. And there is no need to fear things that are different, either. Even if a situation is uncomfortable, everything can be a learning opportunity and a new experience to help you see the world differently.

As a butterfly, admire each flower that you see, and live in awe at the diversity of our world.

7. Let Your Feelings Flow

Life changes will push and pull your heart, bring you from laughter to tears, or even screaming. Sometimes, you will barely recognize yourself, and you will want to hide these parts of you. However, these feelings ARE a part of you, and the worst things you can do is to suppress them or feel guilty for them.

Let your feelings flow. Let your tears, your laughter, your voice, your smiles...let it all flow out of you. Now, you do need to be careful who you express yourself around, because not everyone has your best interests in mind. But those who love you will understand and be supportive where they can be.

One tactic that can help you express these feelings (especially the more painful ones) are to put your feelings into something you can cast away. Write them down and burn the page, paint a rage painting and bury it, or meditate on a rock and throw it far away from you.

8. Make the Small Things Big

If this illness has taught me anything, it's to appreciate the small things. I'd heard that advice many times over the years, but I never fully understood it until I was having to crawl hands and knees to the bathroom because I was in too much pain to walk, or when I would spill my coffee before I could drink it because I had developed a tremor.

So yes, there are things going wrong in life, and they might seem really big...but if you notice the small things that go right, you can make those things big, too. Waking up every day, breathing, walking, or even just having a nice meal...all these things are tiny miracles.

Fill your life with the little beautiful things...and you will find that your life will be full of miracles.

9) An Attitude of Gratitude

Making these little miracles into big things takes the power of gratitude. Sometimes we find ourselves noticing all the things that are going wrong, and it will feel like things are just getting worse. This is because you are training your mind to look for the bad habitually. This might have worked in your caterpillar life, but it will weigh you down and stop you from flying as a butterfly.

You need to learn to keep looking up, and to train yourself to notice the things that make you feel light and happy. The more things you start to become thankful for, the more it will become a habit, and the more things you will find to be happy for every day.

Flap your wings and reach new heights with a light heart...

10. Light Your Candle

Gratitude by itself is not enough. The true power of healing and transformation lies in action. I call this the 'light your candle' concept. And this is how it goes:

If you give a friend a candle as a gift, and they thank you for it over and over, but every time you go over to their home, the candle is just sitting in the corner collecting dust...you will probably not give them any more candles.

However, if you give your friend a candle and they thank you for it only once and never bring it up again, but every time you visit the candle is lit and they seem to use it often...you will know they appreciate it and you will probably give them more candles in the future.

So, when the universe gives you things, and you say thank you and feel grateful, that's good. But what is even better is USING the gifts you are given. LIGHT YOUR CANDLE.

About the Author

Kendra Cordova is a Spiritual Life Coach and Author. Their mission is to help their clients heal through their pain and awaken their spirituality so they can live their best life.

For more, go to: healyourstorywithkendra.com

www.ingramcontent.com/pod-product-compliance
Lightning Source LLC
Chambersburg PA
CBHW071648040426
42452CB00009B/1802